GOD

Lighting My Path

A PERSONAL PRAYER COMPANION BOOK
FOR CATHOLICS

PRAYER JOURNAL CATHOLIC EDITION

ACTIVINOTES

Activinotes
DAILY JOURNALS, PLANNERS, NOTEBOOKS AND OTHER BLANK BOOKS

Date:

Prayer for today

Meditative Scriptures

Special Requests

Answered Prayers

Date:

Prayer for today

Meditative Scriptures

Special Requests

Answered Prayers

Date:

Prayer for today

Meditative Scriptures

Special Requests

Answered Prayers

Date:

Prayer for today

Meditative Scriptures

Special Requests

Answered Prayers

Date:

Prayer for today

Meditative Scriptures

Special Requests

Answered Prayers

Date:

Prayer for today

Meditative Scriptures

Special Requests

Answered Prayers

Date:

Prayer for today

Meditative Scriptures

Special Requests

Answered Prayers

Date:

Prayer for today

Meditative Scriptures

Special Requests

Answered Prayers

Date:

Prayer for today

Meditative Scriptures

Special Requests

Answered Prayers

Date:

Prayer for today

Meditative Scriptures

Special Requests

Answered Prayers

Date:

Prayer for today

Meditative Scriptures

Special Requests

Answered Prayers

Date:

Prayer for today

Meditative Scriptures

Special Requests

Answered Prayers

Date:

Prayer for today

Meditative Scriptures

Special Requests

Answered Prayers

Date:

Prayer for today

Meditative Scriptures

Special Requests

Answered Prayers

Date:

Prayer for today

Meditative Scriptures

Special Requests

Answered Prayers

Date:

Prayer for today

Meditative Scriptures

Special Requests

Answered Prayers

Date:

Prayer for today

Meditative Scriptures

Special Requests

Answered Prayers

Date:

Prayer for today

Meditative Scriptures

Special Requests

Answered Prayers

Date:

Prayer for today

Meditative Scriptures

Special Requests

Answered Prayers

Date:

Prayer for today

Meditative Scriptures

Special Requests

Answered Prayers

Date:

Prayer for today

Meditative Scriptures

Special Requests

Answered Prayers

Date:

Prayer for today

Meditative Scriptures

Special Requests **Answered Prayers**

Date:

Prayer for today

Meditative Scriptures

Special Requests

Answered Prayers

Date:

Prayer for today

Meditative Scriptures

Special Requests

Answered Prayers

Date:

Prayer for today

Meditative Scriptures

Special Requests

Answered Prayers

Date:

Prayer for today

Meditative Scriptures

Special Requests

Answered Prayers

Date:

Prayer for today

Meditative Scriptures

Special Requests

Answered Prayers

Date:

Prayer for today

Meditative Scriptures

Special Requests

Answered Prayers

Date:

Prayer for today

Meditative Scriptures

Special Requests

Answered Prayers

Date:

Prayer for today

Meditative Scriptures

Special Requests

Answered Prayers

Date:

Prayer for today

Meditative Scriptures

Special Requests

Answered Prayers

Date:

Prayer for today

Meditative Scriptures

Special Requests

Answered Prayers

Date:

Prayer for today

Meditative Scriptures

Special Requests

Answered Prayers

Date:

Prayer for today

Meditative Scriptures

Special Requests

Answered Prayers

Date:

Prayer for today

Meditative Scriptures

Special Requests

Answered Prayers

Date:

Prayer for today

Meditative Scriptures

Special Requests

Answered Prayers

Date:

Prayer for today

Meditative Scriptures

Special Requests

Answered Prayers

Date:

Prayer for today

Meditative Scriptures

Special Requests

Answered Prayers

Date:

Prayer for today

Meditative Scriptures

Special Requests

Answered Prayers

Date:

Prayer for today

Meditative Scriptures

Special Requests

Answered Prayers

Date:

Prayer for today

Meditative Scriptures

Special Requests

Answered Prayers

Date:

Prayer for today

Meditative Scriptures

Special Requests

Answered Prayers

Date:

Prayer for today

Meditative Scriptures

Special Requests

Answered Prayers

Date:

Prayer for today

Meditative Scriptures

Special Requests

Answered Prayers

Date:

Prayer for today

Meditative Scriptures

Special Requests

Answered Prayers

Date:

Prayer for today

Meditative Scriptures

Special Requests

Answered Prayers

Date:

Prayer for today

Meditative Scriptures

Special Requests

Answered Prayers

Date:

Prayer for today

Meditative Scriptures

Special Requests

Answered Prayers

Date:

Prayer for today

Meditative Scriptures

Special Requests

Answered Prayers

www.ingramcontent.com/pod-product-compliance
Lightning Source LLC
Chambersburg PA
CBHW080738250626
47170CB00010B/2873